Puppies, Dogs,
and Blue Northers

GARY PAULSEN

Puppies, Dogs, and Blue Northers

REFLECTIONS ON BEING RAISED BY A PACK OF SLED DOGS

HARCOURT BRACE & COMPANY

San Diego New York London

Library of Congress Cataloging-in-Publication Data
Paulsen, Gary.
Puppies, dogs, and blue northers: reflections on being raised by a pack
of sled dogs/by Gary Paulsen.—1st ed.
p.   cm.
Summary: Dog musher Gary Paulsen reflects on the growth—both his own and
the puppies'—as man and animal discover the world.
ISBN 0-15-292881-2
1. Paulsen, Gary—Juvenile literature. 2. Mushers—Minnesota—Biography—
Juvenile literature. 3. Sled dogs—Minnesota—Biography—Juvenile literature.
4. Dogsledding—Minnesota—Juvenile literature. [1. Paulsen, Gary.
2. Mushers. 3. Sled dogs. 4. Dogsledding. 5. Minnesota.] I. Title.
SF428.7.P38P86   1996
798'.8—dc20
[B]   95-18981

The text was set in Dante.
Designed by Linda Lockowitz

First edition
E D C B A

Printed in Singapore

To Lloyd Gilbertson:
Keep the dance going

Puppies, Dogs, and Blue Northers

Love

COOKIE USUALLY HAD puppies easily, but they were always so wonderful and special that I worried excessively each time. Considering that she had five litters of never less than eight pups and twice twelve—altogether over forty pups—this constituted a large measure of worry.

She deserved the effort and concern. Cookie was my primary lead dog for something close to fourteen thousand miles—trapline, training, and one full Iditarod—and had on several occasions saved my life. But more, most important, she threw leaders. Sometimes as many as half her pups tended to lead and a few had, like their mother, become truly exceptional lead dogs; dogs with great, unstoppable hearts and a joy to run. It didn't seem to matter if they were male or female—they were all good.

And so I worried.

This time the breeding had been accidental. We had been on a long training run in early fall, and Cookie had temporarily and with great enthusiasm fallen in love with a big, slab-sided half-hound named Rex. Cookie was running lead. It was a first-snow run—the snow was thin and melting rapidly and would be gone in two days, three at most—and it was so warm (thirty degrees) that I was wearing only a jacket and wool watch cap. We were running at night because of the heat (the dogs were most comfortable at ten or twenty below zero) and I had looked down at something on the sled when the whole team stopped dead.

I knew Cookie was in season and would not normally have run her during her time. But I had young and new dogs—Rex was one of them—and I needed her good sense and steadiness to control them while we ran.

Cookie, overcome by what could only be described as wild abandon, stopped cold, threw it in reverse, and backed into Rex. If he was surprised, he recovered instantly, and before I could react, they were romantically involved.

I pulled the other dogs away from them to avoid any fights, tied them up to trees, and made a small fire to have tea. Usually these things took time—lasted five

or ten minutes—but with Cookie and Rex both in harness she would be anxious and stressful about wanting to run, and I wanted her to see that I had settled in and wanted to remove some of the nervousness so she wouldn't start to fight.

Normally I would have controlled the mating situation better, would have selected a male more to my liking. Rex was very much a question mark. I'd only had him a few days and didn't know much about him, and had I known that this would be Cookie's last litter and that it would be seven of the best dogs—two leaders—that I had ever seen or heard of, I perhaps would have paid more attention.

As it was I ignored them, or tried to. It always seemed to be such a private time for the dogs, the time of mating, and though they were quite open, I in some way felt like an intruder and did not like to watch them.

I turned away and heated snow for tea. The night was still and, consequently, I heard the dogs more than I usually would have. I "heard" the puppies being made.

In truth, much of what dogs are is based in sounds. They are quiet, wonderfully silent, when they run; mile after mile in soft winter nights I have heard nothing but the soft *whuff* of their breath and the tiny jingle of their collar snaps as they trot along.

But almost all other times they live in sound. They bark, whine, wheeze, growl, and—wonderfully—sing.

When they see me come out of the house with harnesses over my shoulder, they go insane, running in their circles, literally bellowing their enthusiasm—some barking, some crying, some yipping, and some emitting a high-pitched keening scream that leaves the ears deaf for hours.

When it rains there is a song, and when it snows or when they want food or when something dies—sad songs, happy songs, duets and trios, sometimes all the dogs trying to harmonize, except the young ones who think they can sing but can't and throw their heads back to try to look adult but sing off-key and with the wrong timing.

They live in sound, always in noise. Perhaps because it is so constant, the art of listening to them falls off, and so many things they say are not heard, are swallowed in the overall sound. (An interesting aside: people know the sounds of their own dogs the way mothers know the cry of their babies. At one checkpoint during the Iditarod during a mandatory layover, some seven or eight hundred dogs were all in an area not much larger than a football field. The din was constant, deafening, and yet if a man or woman inside the building heard the sound of his or her own dog in the cacophony—even if the person was fast asleep—they were up and out the door instantly.)

But this quiet night with the wind gone and even the fire muted somehow by the dark I could hear, and for the first time I think I truly listened to them.

There were some growls, low and soft, envy from the young males who wanted to fight and show they had shoulders and thick necks; quiet whines of interest from others; and then, above all, the soft sounds from Cookie and Rex.

I thought of the word *love.*

There are, of course, many who would dispute it, many who would say dogs simply mate and that only people love, and it is perhaps true that I would have said the same thing before that night.

But the sounds were sweet, soft, gentle—not whines so much as terms of endearment, courtesy, and hope. They made me think of all the good parts of living and loving; how two can honestly become one; how we have made it all seem pointless with posturing and fashion and frills but that it is not frivolous, it is as old and meaningful as time, and it has all to do with the one thing that we are on earth to do—to make more, to make better, to bring new beings into it, into life.

All there, sitting by the fire while two people—I still cannot think of them as dogs—loved and were, in some way that I could not understand, sacred. All there listening to God making puppies.

Nativity

IT CAME IN A WILD STORM, the litter, which did not help to lessen my concern.

I had carefully noted the day when the puppies were conceived and knew that Cookie was as regular as a clock—sixty-five days—when it came to gestation.

But sixty-five days put us smack in the middle of January. January in northern Minnesota is—literally—a hard time. Everything is brittle, difficult. It is paradoxically the very best time to run dogs because it is cuttingly cold—which the dogs love and work best in—and the snow is clean and deep enough to be easy on the sleds.

Everything else is hard. At forty, fifty below, vehicles don't start, tires freeze and break, pipes—even those protected by straw and buried deep—freeze solid.

Hot water must be carried to the dogs, who dehydrate in the dry air of winter, and the old water must be literally chopped out of their pans with an ax. The water is mixed with beef blood to lure them into drinking it fast before it freezes again—within eight or nine minutes—and this process must be done twice a day while running team after team to train for the race and cooking dog food each evening to feed the next day.

And in the middle of January, when it is the busiest, when there is no time, not a minute to spare, and everything is pushed to the absolute limit of its performance envelope—smack in the middle—there came one of the worst blizzards I had ever seen.

It roared down from the North, driven by a dropping cold front called an Alberta Clipper. The winds kicked up to sixty, seventy miles an hour and the true temperature, with driven snow, dropped to forty below—windchill making it close to a hundred below.

Just feeding the dogs became difficult, almost impossible. We had forty-some dogs then and I used a snowmobile to pull a freight sled loaded with dog food out to the kennel and run down the rows of dogs to feed them. It was so dark and the driving snow made visibility so bad that twice I missed the kennel altogether and wound up stuck in the woods west of the dogs. It was the kind of storm you often read about but never see—except this time it was real.

And at the high point, at the very worst peak of the meanest part of the storm, Cookie was due to have her puppies.

My worry turned to something on the edge of panic. She was in her doghouse, her chain disconnected and fresh straw fluffed in, but the storm was so intense I did not see how she could keep the puppies—they are, of course, wet when they come—from freezing solid.

I thought of moving her into the house, but it would be too warm and unhealthy. The dogs' winter coats were in full prime by then, and being in a warm room could do worse than sicken them, it could kill a winter dog to bring him in. The heat would be murderous.

The solution came as I ran the snowmobile past the stack of straw bales by the kennel: If I could not take Cookie to a house, I would bring the house to her.

It was by this time midafternoon and nearly dark, so I left the snowmobile running to use the headlight and carried straw bales to her circle in the kennel.

I constructed a "house" from these straw bales. It took twenty-two bales and a couple of flat boards to hold the roof bales up, but when it was done it was snug and out of the wind and large enough for Cookie and me.

While building I had decided the only way I would get any relief from my anxiety was to stay with her. I smoothed the snow in the bottom of the shelter and spread out fluffed straw almost a foot thick. I had left an igloolike opening just large enough to crawl through, which I could plug with straw after we were inside, then I went to the house and brought a thermos of tea, another of soup, my headlamp, a book to read, my sleeping bag and foam pad, and we moved in.

I had some concern that Cookie would not like it, would prefer her own doghouse, but I needn't have worried. She entered, smelled the straw, peed in one corner to mark it, and made a birth bed in another.

I pulled my gear in, plugged the opening, and unrolled my bag.

"Nice," I said. "Way better than we're used to . . ."

Cookie was busy licking herself and didn't respond—although she usually did. We talked often, sometimes at great length; I frequently explained parts of my life to her, which sometimes helped me understand myself better, and if she didn't know all the words (actually, she did recognize many individual words) she was a master at tones. She could tell by the sound of my voice if I was happy, sad, angry, distracted, worried, unsure, positive, lying, telling the truth, if I truly believed in what I was saying or needed to be argued with to be certain. A hundred, a thousand times a year we "negotiated" differences—when and where to best go— and almost invariably she was right.

And I was not exaggerating when I said it was better than we were accustomed to sleeping in. We had spent years, thousands of miles alone together, camping in rain and open storms, on ice and mud; sleeping huddled under an overhang of snow or dirt or on a frozen riverbed; and sometimes resting by just standing still for a moment—taking a whole night's sleep standing against a tree for four minutes.

An insulated straw house was a palace.

Our combined body heat quickly warmed the inside of the shelter and I feared that it would get too warm. But I opened the straw plug and let some cool air in— kept it at about forty degrees (above zero) and leaned back in the straw to wait for the pups.

Of course, they did not hurry. When you want them to come, they take forever. They only hurry when you aren't ready, never when you are prepared.

I poured a cup of tea and leaned back against the straw, my legs in the sleeping bag, my headlamp adjusted down for reading, and settled in to spend the night with Cookie and Anthony Trollope. I had for some time wanted to read *The Pallisers* and this looked like a good time to at least start.

It had been a long day, however, and the wind tearing by outside and the warmth (a full eighty degrees warmer than out in the wind) made the little bale house seem even more cozy. My eyes closed, opened, closed again, and stayed closed.

I awakened some four hours later. My batteries had run down, so the headlamp gave only a soft glow and for a second I didn't remember where I was; then I heard the sound . . . and knew.

Cookie had decided to go on without my dubious aid and was giving birth. I pulled out of the bag and moved over to her in a crouch.

I'm not sure what I meant to do. She was certainly fine without my help, had done it many times before, and was as I have stated an excellent mother. I was more a hindrance than a help, and I held slightly back to give her room for her work.

She was on the fourth one. The first three—all a gray color like Cookie—were out and cleaned and dry and working at finding a nipple, making the small sounds of new puppies, the tiny whine-grunt that seems to come more from their fat little bodies than their mouths.

The smell filled the shelter. I always thought it smelled new—fresh puppy smell, milk smell, new smell—and I petted Cookie and touched the pups to get man-smell on them so they would come to know it as part of their mother. Many females would not let you touch their pups, would take a piece out of you if you did, but Cookie was milder—at least with me. (I had seen her rip a man's hand when he jumped around the side of her house and said "Boo!" as a practical joke. He took stitches and could never get close to her again without experiencing Cookie's low growl and her lips coming up to show teeth.) But she didn't mind having her puppies handled as long as she could see them.

I picked each pup up, rolled it in my hand to determine sex—although it didn't matter to me which they were. (Females tend to lead better, males usually pull harder—so it all works out.) So far they were all males, and I put them back on nipples and got ready for the next one.

Seven pups, all gray and fat and healthy—little Cookies—all smelling new and milky and warm, and then the eighth and last one came, and it was stillborn.

She worked at it. When I saw she was having trouble I reached in, thinking it hadn't cleared its nostrils or took air too late—I had done miniature CPR on other puppies and gotten them breathing—but it was too late. It must have died in the birth canal or just before, and there was nothing we could do. Cookie licked harder and harder, trying to get it to breathe, her actions becoming more and more frantic.

"It's no use," I said aloud. "This one didn't make it . . ."

She growled concern and it turned to a whine, and

I reached one hand to cover Cookie's eyes and with the other I took the pup and moved it near the door opening. Cookie had never had a dead pup before, but with other females I had done this, hidden the dead one and then taken it away and it had worked. They focused on the live ones and forgot the dead one.

But this was Cookie. I should have known. Cookie was not like other dogs. She was easily the most strong-willed person—and I mean *person*—I had ever met. Once when she'd taken a load of porcupine quills in her face, I'd rushed her to the vet to have her put out so we could pull them, and she simply would not go down. The vet gave her two full doses of anesthetic and it didn't put her out at all. On the third dose she sat, her butt on the table, but was still conscious and ready to bite any hand that came at her. The vet was afraid to give her more, but the drugs slowed her enough so we could pull a quill, then dodge before she hit us.

Stubborn, immensely strong-willed and powerful, and completely, totally dedicated—this wasn't just another dog, it was Cookie.

She looked for the pup with her nose, pushing the others out of the way, tumbling them, trying to find the dead one, and when she couldn't find it, she looked at me.

None of this side-looking stuff, none of this looking up and then away, none of this I-don't-want-tothreaten-you dog-man looks. This was a look from a mother with a missing baby, a look aimed directly, fiercely, hotly into my eyes, into my soul.

Where is it?

It was as clear as if she'd asked it. And I knew that I had almost no time to find the pup and give it back. It was no longer man and dog—if, indeed, it had ever been thus with Cookie and me. It was now mother and intruder, mother and possible kidnapper, mother and fool. She would take me, tear me apart, and there was no doubt anywhere in the shelter. I reached under the straw and started to hand it over, but she reached for it, took it gently in her mouth, and set it on the straw and began working on it again, nudging it with her nose, licking it with hard strokes, trying to get it to breathe, to move, while making small whines. I think she knew, really knew, that it was hopeless but could not let it go, would not let it go.

The other pups nursed and she checked on them at intervals—every two, three minutes—but kept working on the dead puppy and when she could not get it to respond no matter what she did, she picked it up and put it with the other pups to nurse.

She watched it carefully and the movement of the other pups caused the body of the dead one to move and she must have thought it alive because she lay back,

exhausted from the birthing, and closed her eyes and went to sleep.

I waited a full minute, then carefully reached over and removed the dead pup. While Cookie still slept, I crept out of the hut and put the body of the pup some twenty yards away in a snowbank. I didn't want to leave Cookie yet and planned to spend the night or at least stay until I was sure the rest of the pups were all right, and I thought she would not find the body there. I pushed it into the snow and covered it, and then stole back to the shelter, rearranged the plug and unrolled my sleeping bag, and went to sleep. I would take care of the body of the pup when I went to the house.

I had become exhausted and when I next awakened, the wind had abated and I could see daylight coming through the crack in the opening. I turned on my headlamp and scanned the interior of the bale house and saw that Cookie was still fast asleep. I was getting ready to leave when I saw a strange lump.

There, in the middle of the puppies, lay the frozen body of the dead pup, stuck back into a nursing position.

Without awakening me, Cookie had gotten up during the night, gone out, found the pup and brought it back, arranged it to "feed" with the others, and gone back to sleep.

I was caught somewhere between heartbreak and

admiration, and I thought suddenly of orphan children I had seen in the streets in Juárez, Mexico, back in the early sixties and how it would have been for them to have such a mother, such a wonderful mother.

Cookie slept hard, was absolutely sound asleep, and I thought I would take the body now, take it to the house and dispose of it so she could not find it. But when I reached across the hut to get it, her eyes opened and her lips moved to clear teeth, and again she looked directly into my eyes.

I will pull your sled, she said, *and love you and lead the team and save your life and be loyal to all that you are and obey you in all things until I cannot, but if you touch my pup you die.*

I left the pup and it was not for three days, almost four, when the still-frozen pup was clearly not going to come back to life, that she finally surrendered to her grief and let me take it away.

But even then she growled, this time not at me but at the fates, at all of it. That she would lose a young one—a growl at life.

⌒Joy

IT'S WONDERFUL HOW they learn and grow. Puppies.

We did not isolate them from the main kennel as some do, to make them more convenient to handle. Cookie remained loose in the bale house with her litter for three weeks, unchained and able to come and go as she pleased.

During that time all was peaceful. The other dogs understood her "lying in" period, and even when we harnessed and ran other teams, with other leaders, Cookie let us go. Several times she came to the door of the shelter to watch us leave, and I heard her whine once and seem to be discomfited because we left without her. Normally she would not have stood for it. Without puppies to hold her back, it would have been nearly impossible to leave without her, so strong was her drive to run, to lead.

But we weaned early and within nine days started the pups on a meat slurry that was completely disgusting to make—involving shredded livers and kidneys—and so effective it turned even puppies only nine days old into ravenous carnivores. The upshot was that by the time they were three weeks old, the pups were round and fat and didn't need much milk, and Cookie started the weaning process, which varied somewhat depending on location and the litter. In this case she would leave the shelter and sit on top so they couldn't get at her nipples, and only come down to feed them once a day instead of letting them free-feed as she had at first.

The pups—really only just able to trundle around and so fat from her milk and the meat we fed them they could hardly hold their weight up—would rumble around the house in the snow, making pitiful cries, begging Mother to come down and feed them.

By the fourth week the weaning was all but done and Cookie—almost as a signal—would return to the kennel and pick the nearest female and set about trying to kill her. With all her drives, intensity, and strength, she would brook no interference in what she thought of as her territory, and that generally meant the kennel, the house, me and the rest of the family, and all the area encompassed within about a four-hundred-mile radius. She loved us all, but owned us as well.

She did not recognize males as threats to her supremacy, but God help any female when her birthing and nursing period was done. Cookie would imagine some slight or insult and raise holy hell until I put her back on her chain.

This was not a small matter. Cookie was large for a female and was at least a third wolf—with wolf color and wolf markings—and when she hit a dog, it usually went down, and when it was down, she went for the throat, and she had, indeed, on one occasion killed another female in one of these end-of-birthing wars.

As soon as she was on her chain it was all right and she dropped back into her normal frame of reference, where she ran lead and took over the duties of the team again.

But not the puppies. The puppies were left loose to run free until they were four or five months old or until, as my son said, "the day after they get in the chicken coop and kill all the chickens." (It was amazing how often this edict was true; in ten years in the bush, trying every year to raise chickens and turkeys and ducks, we never once got a bird to maturity while we had pups.)

On the whole, we had a very happy kennel, with

dogs that would jump up to be petted and come when called. Sometimes even when it wasn't time to run, my family and I would go and picnic in the kennel, just to be with them, and in a moment of gaiety we put a tape player in a waterproof box in the kennel and kept music going all the time from then on. They liked classical best—some of the females seemed to particularly love Bach—but also favored country music, particularly Willie Nelson. Willie was Cookie's favorite and sometimes—especially during his song "Angels Flying Too Close to the Ground"—she sang with him. What with music, feeding three times a day, watering with warm blood soup twice a day, and all the attention given, the kennel was an obviously happy place.

But to cap it, the loose puppies brought a wild joy wherever they went. I have heard stories of kennels where puppies could not be loose, where other dogs would harm them, and it is possible they are true, but not at ours. I never saw an adult dog harm a pup.

The puppies had a schedule, almost a ritual. They would sleep like they were dead until they smelled the first soup in the morning, then tumble out of the doghouse (the bales were gone and they were back in a normal house) to eat, go to the bathroom, and then head to the first dog of the day, a big bruiser named Charley.

Charley would lie like a sphinx, his great feet out to the front and his head up, while they all ran to greet him and climb all over him. It was a game, all of it, and the rules were very rigid. Apparently Charley was not allowed to move or show expression no matter what the puppies did to him. And the puppies were allowed to do anything they wanted, including hanging on to Charley's lips, which two pups did at one point, swinging like round-bellied little trapeze artists.

When the game was completed with Charley, the litter moved on to the next dog, a frustrated little female named Sarah, who had never had a litter and spent a hectic fifteen minutes trying to get all the puppies in one place at one time so she could "nurse" them. She would grab one, pull it into place, hold it with a foot, then another, then a third, holding them down with her feet, and then it would all go to pieces because when she grabbed the fourth one the first one would get away and she would have to start over. One, two, three, almost four, one, two—it was like trying to grab mercury.

When they all escaped from Sarah, the pups would tumble into Anthony's circle. Anthony, a small dog with amazing stamina, played a game in which he held his head low to the ground and ran around the outside of his circle with the chain stretched tight along the ground. Each dog was held in his or her circle by an eight-foot chain bolted to a rotating car axle driven into the ground in the center and on swivels so it wouldn't tangle.

The chain moving along the ground caught the pups in the middle of their sides and sent them tumbling, and the game was to try to get through Anthony's circle, dodging under the chain or trying to jump over it. Since Anthony was clever and knew how to tighten and loosen the chain—which raised and lowered it—and increase and decrease his speed, very few puppies made it through. But they all tried and must have loved it, because they easily could have walked around Anthony's circle and avoided the whole escapade, but every morning they went to Anthony.

Then to Carlisle, a quick red dog who had wonderful things hidden in his circle—bits of meat, bones with scraps on them, and frozen beaver skulls. (We fed the dogs beaver carcasses given to us by trappers—the state controls the beaver population by trapping because of the damage they do cutting trees and clearing land. There is, indeed, a wonderful and probably accurate theory that all European and many North American cities were initially "settled" by beaver because they cleared areas along rivers where people could start to build.)

Carlisle delighted in hiding the bits of treasure; some under the straw in his house, others in the snow around the edge of his circle, and some beneath him as

he lay. He would roll and laugh and giggle as the puppies descended on him, everybody trying to find the first
and best, digging in his house, around the circle, and
finally diving beneath Carlisle himself for the prizes.

All the adult dogs wanted to be visited by the
pups—males, females, young and old. They loved the
little pack—as they had loved all the puppies we had
raised—and they would reach out and try to snag the
puppies into their circle as they went by, hooking them
with a foot and pulling them in to play and roll, and I
could not watch it without thinking of them all not as
a kennel or a pack but as a wonderfully happy family
with fifty-odd uncles and aunts and brothers and sisters
and parents and grandparents.

The puppies, fat and round and happy, spread an
almost consummate joy wherever they went, and if it
took all morning they would go to every single dog to
say hello and play, at least for a few minutes. Now and
then they would run back to Mother to make sure
Cookie was still there. She would give them each a per-
functory lick—they were no longer just her children but
were weaned and belonged to all and would, in a few
months, be all but ignored by her as she returned to
her normal life—and they would run back and pick up
the trail of fun where they'd left off.

If for some reason the kennel had been an unhappy
one, the puppies on their own would have made it

happy. As it was, they put a joyous frosting on an already merry cake and many times I caught myself laughing out loud as they rumbled through the kennel.

There was a side benefit that was perhaps even more important than the happiness, and that was the education of the pups.

Each dog, young and old alike, had something to teach them, and the pups were avid learners. By the time they were five weeks old they were starting to develop as individuals, which was, and is, completely amazing to me. How one father and one mother could come up with so many completely different beings is perhaps the true miracle of procreation. Some of them were shy, some bold, some smart, and some not-so-smart; some learned in seconds, some took months; some loved with all they were, some were indifferent to all but the sled and pulling. All of them from Rex and Cookie.

But they all learned. At different rates, and most certainly in different ways, they all studied and learned and grew.

Many times—at least once a day—I would catch them at "school." There was often an element of play in the study—as with Carlisle—but sometimes it was very serious. Once while cleaning the kennel I saw them at such serious study. The kennel is cleaned twice daily so the dogs won't eat their own stools (as they will, as wolves do, to recycle any missed food), and the dogs view whoever is doing the cleaning as a servant beneath their consideration. Even the driver, who normally commands a certain automatic attention, is ignored when he approaches with the wheelbarrow, rake, and shovel, and in the ignoring there comes a valuable time to watch the dogs when they do not feel as if they are under scrutiny. It is during this cleaning time that I have seen their humor and anger expressed in natural terms and learned more about them as dogs and not just extensions of human training.

On this one occasion the puppies were with an older dog named William. We never called him Bill, always the more formal name, because he was so staid and proper in the way he sat and studied the kennel and all its surroundings—birds flying overhead, clouds, and, in the summer, butterflies and sometimes ants. I think William, who was large and gray and—like so many of them—wolflike, thought he was on earth for three reasons: to pull and to learn and to teach.

In this case he was trying to teach the puppies the intricacies of anatomy, particularly where it applied to beaver skulls.

Sled dogs are unbelievably strong—perhaps the strongest of all dogs—and much of this strength is imparted to their biting abilities. Once while I was pulling porcupine quills out of William, he reacted and bit the pliers—never me, just the pliers—and actually dented the steel with his teeth. Had he bit my arm it would have come off. But with all their strength and force, beaver skulls are stronger. Beaver regularly chew oak trees down, white and red oak alike, and while their teeth—virtually two wood chisels in front—do the work, the skull carries the weight of leverage when they work.

Inside the beaver skull there are things to eat and the dogs save the skulls and work at getting into them the way a safecracker works at stealing. Now and then a dog would come along who could crush the skull and get inside, but most of them have to find an opening to lick out the interior, and this finding of the openings involves them for days, weeks.

William knew of a way to stick his tongue in the opening left by the spinal cord and lick out the inside of the skull, and was as deft as a surgeon, holding the skull with his paws while licking it clean.

The puppies knew nothing except that the skulls were fun to play with and that—by the smell—there was something delicious inside, and I watched as William tried to teach them how to get into the magic opening.

The puppies squatted in a half-circle around William. He sat like a professor with a beaver skull—minus the lower jaw but with the top front teeth still in place—on the snow in front of him. While the puppies stared up at him, then down to the skull, he leaned down carefully, turned the skull with his paw, and showed the opening where the spinal cord had gone in. Slowly, with great deliberation he leaned down and licked at the opening.

Then he stood again and pushed the skull away with his paw and the puppies piled into it, growling and fighting at the skull, all but a small female—I would later name her Poppy—who had enough of Cookie's intellect genes to have learned. She burrowed beneath the pile of fighting puppies and found the cord opening and stuck her nose into it, then a tongue.

One, I thought. One got it. For a moment I didn't believe what I had just seen. We are so chauvinistic and so brainwashed to humans being superior to all other forms that the ignorance this causes has become something close to horrific. The bullshit—certainly the most appropriate word—about manifest destiny and how we have dominion over all other creatures has caused such terrors as vivisection, cosmetic testing, use of animals (particularly beagles, for some reason) in aerospace testing, and I think ultimately led to such monstrosities as death camps and genocide, which are really nothing more than an insanely rabid expression of one race thinking they are superior to another.

But I was caught in this ignorance, this chauvinism,

and after a few minutes decided that what I had seen was an accident, that I was reading more into it than was really there.

William dispelled that thinking. When it was clear that only Poppy had figured it out and that the others were just playing around, William pulled the skull back, growled at them to get their attention, and started over.

Skull in position, puppies watching, he tipped the skull to show the opening, then, slowly and deliberately, he leaned down to lick the opening in the skull. Then he pushed the skull away and watched them again.

This time Poppy went right for the opening and another puppy—he would be named Marvin by my son—saw her do it and joined her, nuzzling into the small hole and licking inside, and I thought, two.

It is real, I thought. William is teaching them and he has taught two and it wasn't an accident, couldn't be that deliberate and be an accident. And if there was any doubt, William ended it by not being satisfied with only two.

He did it twice more until two more pups had learned and the rest were figuring it out, did it exactly the same, and when he was done he let the pups have the skull as their own and moved back to his house to sit and watch them trying to get into it.

The dogs always left me with wonder, but any further lingering thoughts that I might be superior to them were dissipated by William and his school.

The pups learned in so many ways. There were other direct teachers. I saw a female named Guidon teaching the pups how to clean their feet. She was more pointed and would hold the pup down with one paw while licking at its foot, then wait for the pup to lick at it, turning it over to get at the pad. Again, when I first saw Guidon doing this I thought it might have been an accident, but when she repeated it with several pups, I knew she meant to be teaching them.

Tiny Tim—a hulk of a dog with so much power that he'd once single-handedly pulled a sledge loaded with sixteen *hundred* pounds of dog food forty feet to win a pulling contest (he got the dog food as a prize)— taught them how to step over a chain without tripping. And again, doing it repeatedly and slowly so they would understand how to handle the chain. He would cause his chain to go slack enough to lie on the ground, then step over it carefully, then nudge the pups to do the same. (Tiny Tim was extraordinarily strong; on one occasion a rabbit who could have been either insane or related closely to Evel Knieval ran through the length of the kennel. Or tried to. Tiny Tim slammed against his chain and caught the rabbit, swallowing it nearly whole. When I examined his chain—a chain strong enough to pull a car—I found that he had stretched and flattened the links with his lunge.)

They learned how to dance from a dog named Whippet. Thin and long, she was as lovely as a ballet dancer and did a wonderful loop-over-loop-over-loop dance that made me think of the Bolshoi. The puppies were clumsy, would not get grace and true strength until well into their second full year, but they tried to dance just the same, and in their stumbling imitation of Whippet's elegant demonstrations it was possible to see the grace and beauty of what they would become.

It was when they learned to sing that the puppies became truly hilarious and even the dogs laughed at them.

Puppies can't sing. They want to, they die to sing, but they simply can't. Until they are approaching a year, they can't make the notes work right, can't control their throats or shape their mouths to make the round sound that is so eerie and hauntingly beautiful on a moonlit night.

But they don't know they can't sing. Adult dogs try to teach them, sometimes one at a time, sometimes all at once, and the puppies throw back their heads, their little ears—which don't stand up straight until they are several months old—flopping to the sides and their little mouths trying to make the O shape so important for the song, and they emit a yipping caterwaul that will loosen teeth.

I once watched an adult dog named King wince and go in his house to avoid puppy singing, his head jammed back in a corner and his rear end raised to block the opening in his house to keep the sound out.

But even with the poor quality the singing is infectious, and if one puppy starts and another picks it up the whole kennel usually joins in—perhaps to drown them out—and I have often sung along with them, trying to harmonize, while I was cleaning the kennel.

They learned of harnessing by watching me harness and drive teams, learned of sleds and mittens by chewing on them and stealing them, learned of running by watching the dogs, and learned of love simply because of what they were—puppies—and it is impossible not to love them, even when they are eating your favorite parka that you left on a doghouse for just a minute while you ran to the bathroom.

The Home Wreckers

THE PUPPIES GREW with the kennel, grew with the dogs, became dogs with them—just as I grew and learned and became dog. And in truth, that might have been enough.

But on a cold February morning I saw them watching the house. The kennel was located out in the middle of a forty-acre field, near a line of trees that provided shelter from the wind and shade in the summer afternoons. The house was positioned at the edge of the field, one hundred yards from the kennel, so we could see the dogs but still avoid some of the kennel smell (which was helpful for those people who came to visit who were not accustomed to such things as week-old buried meat and the ammonia from the dogs' urine marking of their houses).

The running trail led out of the kennel and away from the house, back into the forest and up some shallow, long hills into wilderness and, consequently, the dogs rarely came toward the house and, of course, never went inside.

I knew of the dogs, how they lived, what they were, but they didn't know anything of me, of us, except what they saw in the kennel or on a sled.

The puppies changed all that. I saw them sitting as I walked toward the kennel, seven fat little blobs all across the small rise between the house and the kennel, sitting with their heads and ears cocked, watching me come. And when I moved closer I saw they weren't watching me but were looking past me, back at the house, their faces full of curiosity.

"It's the house," I said. "Where we live . . ."

I walked down into the kennel to put antibiotic ointment on a cut one of the dogs had from a minor scuffle and was surprised to see the pups hadn't followed me. Normally they would have been right on my heels but they stayed at the top, watching the house, and when I had finished tending to the dog I walked back past them.

"Come on," I said as I moved by. "Come visit us . . ." I had a thought that it was a shame to waste all that joy on just the kennel, that it would be nice to have them in the yard—just an errant thought—but I didn't really think they'd come.

But they did. It was all very informal at first. They started to tag along but as they moved farther from the kennel and what they thought of as safety they moved slower, two of them stopping and sitting while the bolder ones—the ones who would become leaders—forged ahead. One of the stoppers, later named Crackers, gave a long howl as we moved away, and I stopped and waited. In a moment he started to move again and caught up with us, and that made the other one come and they all followed me to the house.

We had a small home, wood sides, with small windows to reduce heat loss. We heated by wood and also had a wood cookstove and kept dried and canned food from the gardens in the kitchen, including smoked venison, smoked and dried fish, and ropes of garlic. When I opened the door, the aroma that came out always made my mouth water, especially if there was a stew cooking on the woodstove—which was almost all the time—and the same aroma to the puppies, with their elevated sense of smell and taste, must have been irresistible.

As soon as I opened the door the odor caught them—all their noses went in the air, seemed to be caught the way cartoon dogs and cats are caught by odors that pull at them.

"We have company," I said to my wife, Ruth, who was at the stove thawing out a large bucket of meat to feed the dogs.

They trooped in as if they'd been doing it all their lives and hit the house like a horde of huns. Their arrival and enthusiasm—they dispersed in all directions—was appreciated by everyone except Tudor, a large tomcat who had always viewed the kennel as something of a leper colony and thought of the house as very much his private domain. He nailed two of the pups immediately, but they simply changed direction slightly and went around him and kept going.

They were in the house not more than three minutes and in that time pulled all the covers off the beds, tore my son's room apart, ripped a hole in the couch, growled at and then sang with the radio, wagged a greeting to Ruth, ate bits of meat from the thawing dog food, made puddles on the floor, and roared out the door and back to the kennel like a runaway train.

In spite of the damage, all minor, their happiness added to the house the way it did to the kennel and we all decided to make it part of our training program, showing the dogs how we lived.

It was a wise decision because the pups had already arrived at the same conclusion. Early the next morning, while I was lighting fires and taking the night chill off the house, I heard a scratching sound at the door. It was pitch dark and I turned on the porch light to find all the pups on the back step.

We had become part of their ritual, their day. I usually arose first, Ruth and my son Jim staying under the covers until the house was warm, and I opened the door and let them in before I thought of the consequences.

They streamed past me with a wagged greeting and went straight for the bedrooms. I heard screams, thuds, and growls, and four pups went by me, pulling a quilt and blankets, being chased by one extremely irate tomcat and a woman in a flannel nightgown. They made the corner by the entryway, dropped the blankets, slammed against the storm door (I had left the inner door open) and barreled back to the kennel.

"You're up?" I asked Ruth. "The house isn't even warm yet..."

She grabbed the blankets, wrapped herself in them—the kitchen was well below freezing, cold enough so her toes curled under on the linoleum—and without speaking stomped back to the bedroom. Her reaction was not quite as dramatic as the time I dropped the rubber frog on her when she was in the tub—*that* was record breaking; water from the tub could be found in the living room, two rooms away, and the geyser went up so hard it flooded out the ceiling vent fan,

which I had to replace—but it was close and, I decided, well worth repeating.

From then on every morning the pups came, and as they grew and there were other litters, they passed the ritual on to the new ones. All this culminated a year later in what came to be called The Great Kennel Invasion. We had massively expanded our breeding program to prepare for a future Iditarod. In addition, we had bought four litters of puppies from other kennels and our puppies quickly educated them and we were, as people say in the sled-driving business, "getting very doggy."

I went to the door one soft spring morning and there were thirty-six puppies there, waiting to come in.

To show that I am not completely callous, I *did* hesitate. After all, we had a very small house, Tudor was fast becoming neurotic, and Ruth was approaching each morning with something close to paranoia. But they looked so sweet, all atop each other looking up at the door, that I thought, *Oh heck, just this once,* and I opened the door.

Legends, Norse sagas are born this way; marriages are ruined this way; cat lovers are made enemies this way; housework is changed this way.

It was wild. Thirty-six puppies in a small house does not seem like thirty-six but more like two hundred.

There simply wasn't room for them all. Even sitting still they would have filled the place.

But they did not sit still. Every corner, every crack had to be investigated. They hit my son's room first—giving me time to yell a quick warning to Ruth to cover up—and tore all the covers off his bed and then jumped on him, licking and nuzzling, tickling him until I thought he was convulsed and would die. I have never heard anybody laugh so hard. Then they hit Ruth. She had clamped down on the covers and that might have worked with ten, fifteen pups. But this was a battalion and they had the covers off in an instant, climbed on the bed, and attacked the flannel nightgown, the pillows, the wall, digging under and tickling, pushing and pulling until Ruth and Jim were both on the floor covered with puppies and I honestly do not know what would have happened except that one of the pups found the pantry.

A signal, some silent message passed, and they all left the bedrooms and went for it. I grabbed two, put them outside, then two more, put them out, and two and two and two until we thought they were mostly outside only to find there were still two in the back of the pantry, crouched with a venison ham in a dark corner behind the sauerkraut crock, bound and determined to set up permanent quarters.

Puppies.

⌒Young Run

THE PUPPIES GREW, became a year then a year and a half old, and then, finally, became dogs.

We trained by "logging," starting them at four months to get used to the feel of weight pulling behind them. First they get a plain harness to wear around for half an hour each day, just loose and running. Then a four-foot piece of rope is attached to the harness for another few days, and finally a short, light piece of firewood—the "log"—is tied to the rope and they run with that bouncing and skidding along behind them.

They genetically know how to pull, want to run and pull, but going at it slowly lets them build confidence and have more fun in the process.

The first runs with Cookie's last litter were chaotic. I put Cookie on the front, because she is so solid, and then King and William, who are steady and big and do not suffer nonsense.

Then three pups. The pups know what it's all about, had watched us harness a thousand times, and knew what was coming. There was a new four-inch layer of snow on the old snow pack for a cushion and I hooked them all up to a light—fourteen-pound—racing sled with new plastic on the runners.

When I popped the quick-release it felt like the sled left the ground. They flew, the puppies firing up the adult dogs as we roared out the back of the kennel into the woods.

The trick is keeping the puppies running with the sled. They have lived in the kennel, never been out of sight of the adult dogs except to run in the house and wake Ruth, and suddenly they are allowed to run into the forest with the big guys.

There is a whole world to see, to learn, and like all young they want to see and do it all at once. A hundred yards into the woods we spooked a snowshoe rabbit that shot off the trail to the right into a thick stand of red willow.

The pups went after him. And they went with such boundless enthusiasm that they infected the team and we *all* went after the rabbit, even Cookie.

We didn't catch him. We caught willows and trees

and brush and deep snow but we didn't catch the rabbit and it didn't matter.

I pulled everybody back on the trail and we took off again and hadn't gone sixty yards when a red squirrel jumped from the base of a small tree and with the speed of light snaked up a balsam next to the trail.

We went after him. We caught brush and tree limbs and more deep snow and tangled harnesses and our own feet—by this time I was laughing out loud—but we didn't catch the squirrel and it didn't matter.

A quarter mile farther on a mouse blew out of the snow in a small clearing and skittered across the surface before diving back in.

We went after him. The snow was easily three feet deep and the team, pups and all, poised, bounded in the air, and dived beneath the snow, burrowing after the mouse and going so deep they seemed to have disappeared.

We didn't get him. We got more deep snow and grass and the grand sight of a young doe's head poking up through new snow so that it looked disembodied and we got wet and covered in powder but we didn't get the mouse and it didn't matter.

Fifty yards farther along a ruffed grouse got up, thundering in a shower of snow, and the young dogs tried to fly and catch the grouse and I swore for a second they'd make it—Poppy got tail feathers—but they didn't get the grouse and it didn't matter.

We ran for two hours and we saw more mice and deer and grouse and rabbits and birds in the sky and a moose and a car when we crossed the road and a farm dog that ran with us for a while and a coyote and a weasel and a porcupine, and we went after every one of them, laughing and snorting and falling and tumbling, but we didn't catch any of them and it never did matter.

Nothing mattered but the day and the sun and the snow and the celebration of the first glorious run with the young dogs.

Older Run

"Help."

It was, in an impossible situation on an impossible night in an impossible life, the only possible thing to say.

I had never been in such an untenable, completely bizarre situation.

The night had started easy, ridiculously easy, and I should have taken warning from the ease. Generally, when running dogs and sleds, a good moment or two will be followed by eight or nine hours of panic and disaster.

It was early on in training Cookie's pups. They were already trained, knew how to run, where to run, when to run and were having a ball. I was still in that phase of my life when I thought I had some semblance of control over the team, did not yet understand that the dogs ran the show—all of it—and, if I was extremely lucky and didn't hit a tree, I was allowed to hang on the back of the sled and be a spectator. The problem was that my education was coming so slowly that I had fallen behind the dogs—say a couple of years—and it was becoming very difficult to keep up.

This night had begun cleanly, wonderfully. It was midwinter, clear, fifteen or twenty below, a full moon—absolutely beautiful. I put Cookie on the front end and took three of the seasoned dogs and six of the pups, a total of ten dogs, counting Cookie.

Exceeding seven dogs was risky—more than seven dogs meant it would be difficult to stop them or control them, in fact it could not be done unless they wanted to stop—but I knew that and loaded the sled heavily with gear and four fifty-pound sacks of dog meat to help me control them.

Cookie held the gang line out while I harnessed the rest of them, the pups last because they were so excited they kept jumping over the gang line and getting tangled, and when I popped the quick-release holding the sled to a post near the kennel we snapped out in good order.

That's how I thought of it—almost in a stuffy English manner. *Ahh yes, we left the kennel in good order, everything quite, that is to say, quite properly lined up.*

The weight of the sled did not seem to bother them at all. This, of course, should have been a warning to me, a caution that I had exceeded my limits of ability and understanding, but it was a smashing night (still in the English mode), clear and quite, that is to say, quite beautiful, and I gave them their head (as if I had any choice).

We climbed the shallow hills out back of the kennel and moved into the forest. I had a plan to run a hundred miles—take twelve, fourteen hours with a rest stop—and see how the young dogs did with a slightly longer run. They had been to fifty twice and I didn't anticipate any difficulty. If they did get tired, I would just stop for a day and play—God knows I was carrying enough extra food.

I also decided to make it an "open" run and stay away from thick forests or winding trails. Young dogs tend to forget themselves in the excitement and sometimes run into trees on tight corners because they don't remember to swing out. It doesn't hurt them much, but it isn't pleasant and running should, of all things, be fun for them.

So I took the railroad grades. In northern Minnesota there used to be trains through the forests for hauling wood and supplies to the logging camps and to service the hundreds of small towns. Most of the towns are gone now, and much of the wood is hauled on trucks, but the railroad grades are still there.

In a decision so correct it seems impossible that government could have made it, they decided to pull the tracks and ties off the embankments and maintain them for wilderness trails. In the summer they use them for bicycles and hikers, in the winter for skiers and snowmobilers and now dogsledders.

The trails make for classic runs. It's possible to leave the kennel and run a week, hundreds and hundreds of miles, without seeing the same country twice.

The one problem is the trestles. Minnesota is a land of lakes and rivers and every eight or ten miles the trains would cross a river. They made wooden trestles for the tracks and the trestles are still there. They are open, some of them sixty or seventy feet high, and bare wood—although they took the tracks themselves off so it was possible to see down through the ties.

Because they were open they would not hold snow so the snowmobile clubs covered them with one-inch treated plywood to close them in and provide a base for the snow.

The first few times we crossed one, the dogs hesitated, especially on the higher ones, but I took it easy and the older dogs figured it out and passed confidence to the team and it worked all right.

We had by this time run the trestles many times,

knew where each one was, and the dogs whizzed across when we came to them.

Until now.

Twenty-five miles into the run, smoking through the moonlight, we came to a trestle over an open rushing river. I had turned my headlamp off to let them run in the moonlight, which they preferred, and was thinking ahead, way ahead, of a place we were going to camp to rest the pups. It was one of the most beautiful places I had ever seen, a quiet brook kept open by small warm springs, winding through a stand of elegant spruce and tall Norway pines. It was a place to make you whisper and think of churches, and I liked to stop there and sit by a fire, and I was thinking of how it would be to camp there and be peaceful when the dogs suddenly stopped.

Dead in the middle of the trestle.

I hit the brake with my right foot and almost killed myself. Some maniac had come and stolen all the plywood from the trestle and when I jammed the two hardened steel teeth of the brake down instead of sliding on the plywood surface to a gradual stop, they caught on an open cross tie and stopped the sled instantly.

I, however, did not stop.

In a maneuver that would have looked right in an old Mack Sennett comedy, I slammed into the cross handlebar with my stomach, drove all the wind out of my lungs, flew up and over the sled in a cartwheel, hit to the right of the wheel dogs, bounced once on the iron-hard cross ties of the trestle, ricocheted neatly into space, and dropped twenty feet into a snowbank next to the river, headfirst, driving in like a falling arrow.

All of this occurred so fast I couldn't mentally keep up with it and still somehow thought that I must be on the sled when I was upside down in the snowbank. As it was I had hit perfectly. Had I gone a few feet farther I would have landed in the river and probably have drowned or frozen, ten feet sooner and I would have missed the snowbank and hit bare packed ice, which would have broken my neck. It was the only place for me to land and not kill myself, but at the moment I was having trouble feeling gratitude.

I pushed my way out of the snow, cleared my eyes—it had happened so fast I hadn't had time to close them and they were full of snow—and peered up at the underside of the trestle where I could look through the ties and see the team still standing there, the dogs balanced precariously, teetering over open space.

"Easy," I called up. "Just easy now. Easy, easy, easy . . ."

Cookie had hit the trestle without stopping and run out, thinking that's what I wanted, until the whole team was out on the open ties. What stopped her was the pups. Somehow the adult dogs had kept up, stepping on ties as fast as possible to keep going, but the young dogs had less experience and had tripped and gone down. Thank heaven they weren't injured and Cookie stopped when she felt them fall.

But the problem was still there. The team was spread along the trestle, each dog on a tie, and it seemed an impossible situation. To swing a dog team around requires a great deal of space. If they are dragged back on top of each other they get dreadfully tangled and tend to fight, and I couldn't imagine a dogfight at night with ten dogs on a narrow railroad trestle twenty feet off the ground.

An answer did not come to me immediately. I climbed the bank back up onto the trestle. Cookie was frozen out in front of the team holding them, her back legs jammed against one cross tie and her front feet clawed on the one in front, and the snow hook had fallen in the impact of the stop and had set itself in the ties under the sled so the team was held in place while I decided what to do.

I couldn't turn them around.

I couldn't drive them over the trestle without in-juring dogs.

"I can't do anything," I said aloud to Cookie, who was looking back at me waiting for me to solve the thing. "It's impossible . . ."

You, her eyes said, *got us into this, and you'd better get us out.*

Her message hung that way for half a minute, my thoughts whirling, and I finally decided the only way to do it was to release each dog, one at a time, and let them go forward or backward on their own. I thought briefly of carrying them out, one by one, but I had no extra rope to tie them (it was the last run I made without carrying extra rope) when I got across the trestle.

I would have to let them go.

I started with the older dogs. I let them loose and set them on the ties and was amazed to see that each of them went on across the trestle—the longer way— rather than turn and go back. They didn't hesitate but set out, moving carefully from tie to tie until they were across. Whereupon they didn't stop and instead, as I had feared, took off down the railroad grade. They had been here before and knew the way home. I let the young dogs go then and they were slower and more frightened, especially when they looked down, but as soon as they crossed they took off as well and vanished in the night as they tried to catch up with the rest of the dogs.

"Well," I said to Cookie. "It's you and me . . ."

I let her loose and was amazed to see her take off after the team. We were good friends, had been for years, and I was sure she would stay with me, but she was gone in an instant.

"Traitor." I said it with great feeling. The truth is she could not have pulled the sled anyway. It was too heavy for one dog. But it would have been nice to have company. I worried that they would have trouble, get injured somehow, run out on a highway and get hit by a car.

It was like watching my body leave me, my family, and I gathered up the gang line and unhooked the snow hook and dragged the sled across the trestle. Once I got it on the snow it slid a bit easier and I thought that it must be thirty, thirty-five miles to home the shortest way and it would take me three days—or three miserable days, as I considered it then. I had a thermos of tea on the sled and I took time to have a cup, feeling at intervals sorry for myself and hoping silently that I would someday meet the man who stole the plywood from the trestle.

I was putting the inevitable off and I finally accepted it and put away the thermos and moved to the front of the sled and put the gang line around my waist and started pulling. Once I broke it free it slid well enough and I set a slow pace. I had thought of hiding the sled in some way and coming back for it later but it was coming on a weekend and the snowmobilers would be on the trails and there were hundreds of them. Surely the sled—boiled white ash and oak with plastic runner shoes—would be too tempting.

I pulled half an hour on the embankment, trudging along—it seemed like a week—and I developed an updated gratitude for the dogs; their effortless strides covered miles so fast that I felt like with my own puny efforts I was on a treadmill. It seemed to take ten minutes to pass a tree.

Fifteen more minutes, I thought, *then I'll take a break.* I had also decided to throw out some of the dog food and let the wolves have it. It was commercial meat and had cost money but at the rate I was moving I wouldn't get it home until I was an old man anyway.

Ten minutes passed and I said to heck with it and sat down on the sled and was sitting there, sipping half a cup of tea, when I heard a sound and Minto, a large red dog who had a pointed face, came trotting up and sat down facing me.

"Hello," I said. "Get lonely?"

He cocked his head and I petted him, and while rubbing his ears another dog, named Winston, trotted up.

"What is this?" I asked. "Loyalty?"

The truth is they shouldn't have been there. I had lost dogs several times and had them leave me and run home. Trapline teams, or teams that are lived with and enjoyed recreationally, sometimes are trained to stay with the musher; and indeed Cookie had brought a team to me when I was injured once while trapping. But that is rare. Mostly they go home. And race teams, trained for only one thing, to go and go and never stop, simply do not come back. These were not trapline dogs but race dogs, and while I sat marveling at them four more came back, then one more, then the last two pups and, finally, Cookie.

I stood and spread out the gang line and hooked up to their harnesses, which were still on the dogs, putting Cookie in first and then the rest, and I wanted to say something and I finally did manage to get "thank you" out. But in truth I couldn't speak. I had a lump the size of a softball in my throat. I stood on the back of the sled and they lined out and took off and I still wondered how it could be.

I do not know what happened out there—although some of the dogs had slight wounds in the end of their ears clearly made by bites. I did not see nor could I even guess what had transpired.

I know how it looked. I had been alone, Cookie had run after them, and they had come back. All of them, some bleeding slightly from bitten ears. They all got in harness and we finished the run in good order and when I was sitting in the kitchen later, sipping a cup of hot soup and trying to explain it to Ruth, I shook my head.

"I know it sounds insane but it looked like Cookie went after them, caught them, and sent them back to me. I've never heard of anything like it."

"Well, if it looks like a duck, quacks like a duck, and walks like a duck . . ."

I nodded. "I agree, but it's so incredible."

"I don't know about that, but I do know one thing."

"What's that?"

"You aren't paying her nearly enough . . ."

Last Run

THE STORM WAS WILD, torn from the belly of the Arctic
north by two-hundred-mile-an-hour jet-stream winds
and dumped down on Minnesota like a scourge. Trees
were frozen and exploded when they could not contain
the expanding moisture within, the wind snapping them
away like straw. Cattle were found dead, deer frozen
stiff, horses and moose killed, and people, always some
people caught out in it to lose fingers and toes and ears
and, for those who were drunk, to die, frozen in a ditch
or in their car only ten, fifteen, twenty yards from the
house. One young woman is found frozen so solid they
cannot get a needle into her arm and somehow, in some
miracle nobody understands, she lives with only a finger
gone while a mile away a man dies in his car, warm as
toast, from carbon monoxide that leaks up through the

floor because he is drunk and doesn't know enough to clear away the snow.

Cookie and I sit in the living room watching television.

These things have happened:

On a run not too long in the past Cookie started to limp. I rubbed her feet and looked for cuts and even used a magnifying glass and could find nothing, but the limp persisted. She favored both back legs. I gave it four days without running and when it didn't go away, worrying, I took her to the veterinarian.

He tested and retested and took X rays and came out of the room and shook his head.

"What is it?" I asked.

"Arthritis. She has a mild case in her back ankles. She'll be fine if you don't run her."

Don't run her? We had so many miles together, so many rivers and lakes and hills and mountains—she had led for a whole Iditarod, all the way to Nome from Anchorage. I couldn't imagine not looking up and seeing Cookie.

"Are you sure?" I asked.

He nodded and held up the X ray. "See here, at the ankle? See this swelling? You'll have to retire her, use another leader."

I sighed and nodded. "I have some others but I've always run her . . ."

"Not anymore."

And so she retired. It was not easy. I took her out of the kennel and moved her to the house. She had been in the house on only one occasion, when she ate an entire box of Cheerios, swallowing it nearly whole, a partial roast on *top* of the refrigerator, a full pound of butter in one gulp, and had a leather glove with meat smell on it halfway down her throat when I finally got her outside.

It took some time to get her adjusted to the newness and temperature. I took her around the yard, introduced her to the chickens (those that had miraculously lived past the puppies), one yard cat, though I couldn't find the other, and then I brought her in the house, where I gave her an introduction to Tudor. This did not go well and Cookie wore the scars of the introduction for the rest of her life, although an uneasy truce was held from then on.

I made an initial mistake by thinking generically. I assumed it was all right to show Cookie one cat and tell her "NO!" in a stern voice and she would understand that meant for all cats, the same with chickens and house dogs. I was wrong. Cookie was more specific and the next morning the cat I had not introduced her to was gone. We looked for it for a day and more until I saw a pile of Cookie's stool with the cat's collar in it and knew what had happened. After that I made certain to show her each and every thing she was not supposed to do.

We had by this time accumulated quite a menagerie other than the sled dogs. We loved dogs in general and people knew this, and almost any dog that was not wanted found its way (often mysteriously left at our door) to our home. We had a small terrier, a Chihuahua, a Border collie, a half-Lab, a rottweiler, a, nondescript farm breed, and a small yellow mutt. Cookie had to meet each of them, understand that each of them was protected and allowed to live in the same house. Once she figured it all out, she moved in.

It was still not without some difficulty. Cookie had always been the number-one dog and knew it. When she came into the house she "marked" (peed) in the corner of each room to establish her territory, which did not exactly endear her to Ruth. But after some time Cookie learned she could only mark in one spot and I kept a paper there that I threw out immediately afterward.

"It's this way," Ruth said when it all seemed to be settling down. "As long as everybody—and I do mean *everybody*—does exactly as she tells them to do at every moment of every day and every night it will be all right."

"That's how I see it," I said, watching Cookie walk

through the kitchen and make Tudor hit the top of the refrigerator and stick to the ceiling. "Pretty much."

"Well, good then," she said, nodding. "Just so I know . . ."

I went ahead and ran dogs with other leaders, trained for what I hoped would be my next Iditarod. Cookie had some trouble when she heard me harnessing for those first few runs. Ruth said she nearly tore the house apart trying to get out the first time. But Ruth gave her bits of meat and other treats—she had developed a taste for peanut brittle, which we made often— and after the fourth or fifth run, when she heard me harnessing she just trotted into the kitchen to get a piece of peanut brittle from Ruth and went back to her cedar-shavings bed.

The training went well, or seemed to, but after a few months I climbed into the middle of one whale of a fight between Minto and William, who had both fallen in love with Frenchy, a little Canadian female given to me by a trapper.

I grabbed each of them and pulled them apart. They fought to get back at each other and I pulled harder and felt a sudden pain in my chest. I had once ripped my sternum loose and I thought that's what had happened.

The pain went away, but a week later I had to fly

to Boston on business and in the Boston airport for no apparent reason the same pain came back and this time I knew what it was. The tests proved positive. I had heart disease, and the doctor told me almost the exact thing the vet had told me about Cookie.

"You'll have to hang it up and not run the dogs anymore . . ."

And so I retired with Cookie. Initially I had the idea that my life would be sedate. I found someone to take the dogs (and he is still running them) and I moved into the house. I mistakenly thought I would have to sit a lot, and for the first time in eight years I bought a television set and a satellite dish to help pass what I thought would be monotonous hours. The truth was I couldn't watch it. I tried. I would sit on the couch and turn the thing on in the evening and Cookie would come and sit next to me—she *loved* it and kept trying to look in back of the set and see where the people were—and we would try to watch it together. I had come to know greater things in my life, however, and television had become so appallingly awful that I simply couldn't watch it (and still can't).

So I sat and wrote notes in longhand with an old fountain pen for books I hoped to write, while Cookie watched, growling if somebody came to sit too close to me and lifting her lip if a dog or cat appeared on the screen. The months passed and we evolved from friends

who had run thousands of miles together to friends who would sit and talk together. She stayed with me constantly, wherever I went in the house. Even the bathroom. If I locked her out of a room she tore at the door until I would open it, then she would come in and sit near me—eating, resting, bathing. Wherever. If I went outside she followed, each time I left, even for an armload of wood. When I sat and read—which I did more and more—she would sit nearby, or lie down and half sleep, one ear cocked to hear if I moved or said anything. And so we spent our days and I thought we would continue to spend them.

It had been months since I'd let the dogs go and some of the grieving at losing the kennel and team had abated, or the edges had dulled.

I assumed the same had happened to Cookie. She seemed to love lying around watching television, walking with me to the mailbox to get the mail—a daily event—and sitting on the back porch and watching the loons come back from whatever mysterious southern world they go to in the winter. Summer passed and the grass grew back where the kennel had been and a neighbor farmer plowed and disked and planted alfalfa where the pups had run. By early fall, when the alfalfa was knee-high, the last signs of the kennel were obliterated and visually, at least, it seemed there had never been the noise and joy of the dogs.

But for two things . . .

There came the first hard fall morning. I arose early—the diet and exercise and medication had helped and I was becoming more active; not as I had been but better all the time—and I went out for wood for the stoves. Cookie, of course, went with me. She had slept next to my side of the bed, arose with me, and followed me into the bathroom and watched while I brushed my teeth and dressed and then, of course, followed me outside.

The fall color was in full bloom and the oaks and maples and poplars around the house and the field looked like a garish impressionist painting. To say it was beautiful was an understatement—it was very nearly in poor taste, the colors so loud and vivid they cut the eyes, went into the mind.

There was, for the first time in the year, a snap to the weather. Not bitter cold but just that, a snap, enough to sting the cheeks and ears and fingers. I walked to the woodpile to split kindling for the wood-stove and Cookie accompanied me. But at the pile I stopped and she kept going.

Out, into the field, to where the kennel had been. I watched her go and knew what she was thinking. First long runs came with first cold, the first real reaches, and Cookie used to love them, loved to take off when there was not always the possibility of coming home. I called her but she ignored me and kept going, and I put the ax down and followed her out into the drying alfalfa stubble. There was, literally, no sign there'd ever been a dog there, let alone seventy or eighty of them. The neighbor had plowed and eradicated any indication, but Cookie knew exactly where everything had been. She went to the precise spot where she'd stood so many hundreds, perhaps thousands, of times, where she had waited in harness for the rest of the dogs to be harnessed and hooked up, and looked back as if expecting dogs to be there, ready for the first long run, the beginning of fall.

"No," I said, coming up next to her. "There aren't any."

She looked up at me, then back to the rear, and whined softly.

"We don't do that now. Come, come with me back to the woodpile."

I walked off and beckoned but she hung back, stayed for another thirty or forty seconds, a minute—it seemed an hour—and I would have gone back to coax her but I would have lost it. It took everything in me to keep walking and not look back at her standing there waiting, and when at last she caught up with me, still whining, I reached down to pet her and she leaned in against my leg.

I thought that was the last time the memory would

bother her but I was wrong. There was to be one more time. She would rise one more time, and it came during a storm.

Fall had surrendered to winter not with a blast but with a whimper, easing in to soft rain and low gray days, turning gradually to slushy snow and never the clean, hard brittle beauty that was northern winter.

Until the storm.

We were secure. The house was tight, there were sixteen cords of oak cut and split nearby, the chimneys were clean, the pantry full of good—vegetarian—food. Even Tudor, normally upset by weather, had settled in for winter and sat on the back of the couch, one eye warily on Cookie because he still didn't trust her, staring out at the wind ravaging the trees and driving snow sideways.

Cookie asked to go out. She had become—except for marking her paper daily—the model of cleanliness and was housebroken to a fault, and she went to the window and put her feet up on the sill and whined and looked out and then moved to the door, and without thinking I let her out.

But it was not because she had to go to the bathroom. Not this time.

We had always run to storms. I am not certain how it started but at some point early on in our training, either consciously or subconsciously, I had decided that the worse the weather, the better it was for training. In a way it made sense because nothing in Minnesota—not the very worst storms I have ever seen—could prepare us for the storms and winds in the interior of Alaska, where I have seen people literally blown off their sleds and cartwheeling out across the tundra. But the upshot of this all was that whenever it got bad we ran, and Cookie had learned this as a pattern and I had forgotten it.

When I let her out I always watched because her arthritis was acting up and she had trouble walking. I expected her to hit the yard, get her business done, and come back in the house. But she didn't do anything I expected. Instead she smelled the wind, stood for a moment, wheeled and headed back for what used to be the kennel.

"Darn," I said.

"What?" Ruth was by the stove with a cup of coffee.

"I have to go out . . ."

"In this?"

I found my parka and, bundled with the hood up and tied, staggered out into the wind and into the open field, where the gusts almost blew me over. The snow was new and nearly a foot deep but Cookie's tracks were already filled in. It didn't matter because I knew where she was going and had been there so many times I didn't need to see the direction.

I found her in the same place, standing alone in the kennel in the harnessing position, waiting, the wind tearing at her, her nose up and into the storm, smelling, knowing what we had to do, waiting for me to harness her and the dogs.

I stood next to her and petted her neck and held her there while the wind and storm came at us and she whined, a soft sound barely over the howl of wind, and I shook my head so she could see it.

"No," I said. "It's done now, it's all over—no more runs."

And that time she understood. She leaned against my leg as she had done so many times so I could pet her head and the whine ended then, for the last time the whine to run, the beg to run, and I started back for the house and she walked with me and didn't need to be convinced.

Two more summers and one more winter went by while I kept to my diet and somehow got better and Cookie took the yard, owned it, and owned the house and became part of my new life as she had once been part of the old, of the runs, the long runs.

And then one morning, a soft morning in late summer, I let her out and she did not come back in for breakfast, to be with me, to be close to me. After a cup of tea I went into the yard and called her. It was the first time in those years since I had been home that she had not been with me for any length of time, and when she did not come to my call I knew, I think, but I looked anyway. I found her under the spruce tree, her face to the east, dead with her eyes half open.

I sat for a time next to her, crying for her and mostly in self-pity because I would have to live without her now, and then I took her back to the place in the kennel where she loved to stand, the place where we harnessed, and I buried her there with her collar still on and the little metal tag that had the number 32, her number (and mine) in the Iditarod, and after a long time I went back to the house and sipped tea and thought of when she was young and there was nothing in front of us but the iceblink on the horizon, and I hoped wherever dogs go she would find a lot of good meat and fat and now and then a run.